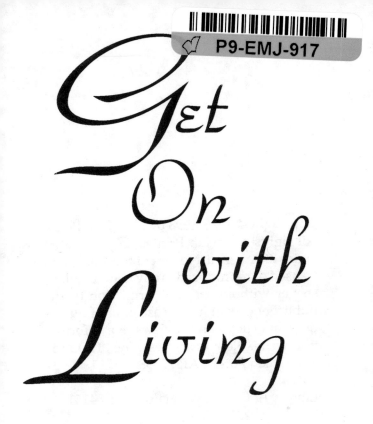

Get On with Living

SIMON SCHROCK

New Leaf Press

Library of Congress Catalog # 93-84141
ISBN: 0-89221-233-0

Cover Photo by: J & J Tiner Photographs

Preface

What is life all about and why am I here? What do I want to become? Do I want to serve or be served? Whom shall I serve? As I look at these questions, I need answers. To get on with living I must know why I am here, whom I am committed to serving, and who leads my life.

Many times people say, "If only I could live my past over, I'd be different. I would live life with a more correct behavior." I catch myself entertaining the same thoughts. But life, like a spoken word, cannot be re-lived. We must move on to living from where we are. We are free to change our future, free to examine our commitments, free to look at our priorities. I've discovered that agonizing over the past, nursing bitterness over failures, and missing out on relationships with others prevents me from joyfully living life now.

It is easy to get stuck in the groove of the everyday grind. We may be unaware that life has become miserable because of being stuck in bitterness and resentment. The good news is that there is forgiveness for the past. We are invited to live now. Let's get on with living the way we were designed to live.

In these chapters are principles I need to apply in my life in order to experience fulfilled living. I am deeply grateful to those persons who have helped me in my discovery of these principles for living. I trust that what has been helpful to me will be an encouragement to you for living your life as I share with you in this book.

— Simon Schrock

Foreword

Don't look now, but there's a long line of people following you (and perhaps gaining on you).

There. Steal a glance. They have the look of experts, right? Experts who are willing and eager to live your life for you. Give them a pinch of attention and they'll take a mile of liberty with your future.

Look them over. There are gurus offering instant insight, pop psychologists eager to certify you okay, religious enthusiasts with the answer to everything. Perhaps your parents are in the line, bent on your fulfilling their sense of unlived life, scripting your job, your future, your destiny.

There are more than enough experts to go around. I'm not shopping for them. I doubt if you are either. What I need are models — persons who are living in real, effective, vital ways.

I find I'm looking for them all the time, these persons who "model" life. And I feel a flush of joy when I find a model who embodies integrity, loving relationships, and living with rich freedom.

"Models" recommend nothing they have not already tried or are now experiencing themselves. So they live their faith, demonstrate their values, act their convictions, embody their beliefs. They're whole persons.

Such models don't snap out easy directions, but they are directing their lives toward meaningful goals. They are directed by a vision that is greater than themselves and their own personal success or happiness. They are direct and explicit in what matters most to them. So they are — truly are — living by their own directions.

Such models don't live with a risky instability but they risk staking their lives on the central truths they have come to value deeply. They risk being open and vulnerable in spelling out what these central truths are. They risk being challenged by others to change, to grow, to repent. So they are — truly are — risk-taking people.

Such models don't get hung up on little things but they are concerned about the simple things of life. They see the little things of daily relationships as crucial things, for in them the real issues of life unfold. They see the truly simple things as being the most profound. So they are — truly are — persons of deep simplicity.

Such models are unafraid of being unique. They are who they are without apology or defense. They do not ask that you imitate them, but that you discover your gifts, your ministry, your place of service and witness. That's where the joy emerges. They call you to the enjoyment of discovering your uniqueness as a child of God.

All this is cause enough for a feeling of joy. And I'm feeling it as I read these chapters from the life of a man I've come to respect and appreciate. He models what discipleship — following Jesus daily in life — is about in the routine of work in a major urban setting. He goes public with his values and life, as a witness. Read on, and be a fellow witness.

— David Augsburger

Contents

1. First, Read the Directions 13

2. Pay the Price — It's Worth It! 19

3. Confess — Repent — Grow 25

4. Find the Right Church 29

5. Be Faithful Where You Are 35

6. Challenge Your Own Convictions ... 41

7. Give Yourself 47

8. Be Sure Your Pilot Knows
   How to Fly 51

9. Follow God, Not "Sarah" 57

10. Forget It? No, Forgive It! 65

11. Put the Put-Down on Pride 71

12. Don't Live by the Advertisements ... 77

13. Stop Fussing and Build
    Something! 83

14. Help Stop the Tragic Devaluation ... 89

15. Establishing Friendships at the
    Line Fence 95

16. Have a Healing Ministry of
    Your Own 103

17. Take Courage from John 111

18. Get On with Living 117

19. Would You Feel at Home
    in Heaven? 123

1

First, Read the Directions

"This blender is no good!" you tell the appliance store clerk. "I've had it only a week and now it won't even run. I want my money back!"

The clerk examines the appliance briefly, points out the problem, and asks, "Did you read the directions?"

"Well, no," you admit sheepishly.

We do it that way many times. After everything else fails we read the directions. The makers supply the directions, and they should know how their product works. It is best to follow the original designer's instructions.

The same thing applies to human beings. They, too, have an original Maker, and they work best and are happiest when they follow their Maker's directions. Before living life one should read the directions so he can live life at its best.

Many persons live their lives according to their own desires. They waste their lives by trying to live without reading the directions. Some turn to the directions after their own way fails. Others live out their entire lives without ever reading the instructions.

God designed people. He gave them specific directions on how to live. These directions are found in the Bible. To move toward real living you should read the original Creator's directions

In Jeremiah 5:25 the prophet said, "Your sins have withholden good things from you." When a person finds the "good things" in life, living becomes an exciting adventure and a meaningful journey. The route to the good things is found in the directions — the Bible.

But God didn't only *tell* us how to live, He also came and *showed* us how in the person of Jesus. "I am come a light unto the world" (John 12:46). "I am the way, the truth, and the life" (John 14:6). "Christ also suffered for us, leaving us an example, that ye should follow his steps" (1 Pet. 2:21).

God knew we humans couldn't make it on our own. He knew we would take our own way. As the Bible says, "We have turned every one to his own way" (Isa. 53:6).

The directions point out clearly that we are taking our own way and following the path of sin. We are sinners. In fact that is why God came in Christ. After living out the directions of life, He gave His own life as a sacrifice to pay for our sins. "For he hath made him to be sin for us, who knew no sin; that we might be made the righteousness of God in him" (2 Cor. 5:21).

God's directions call for us to come to Christ, confess our sins, and trust Him to forgive them. "If we confess our sins, he is faithful and just to forgive us our sins, and to cleanse us from all unrighteousness" (1 John 1:9). After we experience forgiveness we can get on with real living as the Bible directs.

Not only did the original Maker show us and tell us how to live, but He will also come into our lives in the person of the Holy Spirit, "Even the Spirit of truth . . . for he dwelleth with you, and shall be in you" (John 14:17).

When you honestly invite Jesus to come into your life — to live it for you — the Holy Spirit baptizes you into the family of Jesus. You are born of the Spirit. He dwells in you.

He is in you to help you live the directions of your original Maker. He helps you to live on the road that leads to heaven.

Many people try to live on their own. They hope to become a success in the eyes of the public, reach the top in achievement, and take the honors for themselves. They live their lives to gain status in the world and accumulate wealth for security and acceptance. However, they discover they are not really happy. Their riches do not satisfy.

As a result of their disillusionment with life, some persons turn to drugs, alcohol, or perverted sex. For some it is suicide. Others turn to the directions of life, yielding to Christ, and getting their lives to go straight.

I know a family who went through this process. They became dissatisfied with life the way they were living it, so they started to read God's directions. They got a completely new outlook on life. They asked Christ to forgive their sins, and now they are living a new life in the Spirit.

As they read God's directions for living — the Bible — the Holy Spirit helps them understand it. Since God's Holy Spirit lives in them, He gives them power to live out the directions in daily life. Now they have power to love instead of hate, respect the other person instead of envy, give instead of demand, and return kindness instead of cruelty. They have made a change in their life, their attitude toward work, their value of money and possessions. To put it simply they love God and have a love for their fellow man. They are discovering how to live life the way it was meant to be lived in the first place.

God created people. He came in Jesus to live among us. He gave us directions for living in the Bible. To the persons who choose to live for Him and follow His directions, He gives the presence and power of His Holy Spirit to live a rich and meaningful life for God.

So what will you do with life — live it on your own, or follow your Maker's directions? It's your life — you may choose your way to live it. But your Maker's directions are the best guide for life, and the only way to an eternal home.

So get on with living — but don't forget to read and study the Maker's directions.

2

Pay the Price — It's Worth It!

Jesus began His ministry by calling people to follow Him. He said to Andrew and Peter, "Follow me" (Matt. 4:19). That call has been going on ever since. Today His Spirit is calling people to follow Him and carry on His work. Jesus said, "He that taketh not his cross, and followeth after me, is not worthy of me" (Matt. 10:38).

What does it mean to follow Jesus and be His disciple? For Andrew and Peter it meant leaving the fishnets and accepting another way of life. What does it mean for us to be disciples today? What is the price of discipleship?

Let's say you are a Jewish boy. You were taught the laws of God and that the Messiah would soon come. You go through Jewish school, attend the synagogue every Sabbath, keep the holidays, and deeply treasure your bar mitzvah service. Your ties are close to your family. Then contact with a follower of Jesus happens. You are told of Christ's love, death, and Resurrection. He was "wounded for our transgressions" (Isa. 53:5). You yield your life to Jesus and trust Him as a sin-forgiver. The news reaches your family. You are an outcast — rejected as a son. A mock funeral is held for you. Would you follow Christ if that were you?

For a Jewish person to become a disciple of Jesus often means rejection by his family, loss of all he holds dear, and a complete change of living. It is a costly thing for a Jew.

Another example: Suppose you lived in a country that forbade public expression of religion except at the government-approved church. As a result of Christians privately sharing with you, you become a follower of Jesus. You ask to be baptized into their fellowship of believers. You are in the meeting, and just as you are being baptized some strangers break through the door. You are captured, imprisoned, and tortured — because you chose to follow Jesus. Can you imagine being a follower of Jesus like that?

For some people following Christ means taking a chance with their lives. They know the cost of discipleship is high. For others, sacrifice of self is the price they pay.

What does it mean to the twentieth-century American to follow Christ? Often it seems, the American image of a Christian is that of someone from a good family who bothers no one, has a good income, provides well for his family, and pays his church dues. He gives his out-of-style clothes to the Salvation Army, and thanks God once a year for his "freedom in a Christian nation." He occasionally occupies a pew and smiles at the pastor as he goes out the door.

Is that being a disciple? No! That makes Jesus too cheap. He is not just a blesser of our system. Following Him is not having Him bless our wealth and approve of our self-indulgence while the rest of the world suffers. He is another way of life. He is another kingdom.

Being a disciple is more than a TV star referring to God at the end of a show. It's more than thanking God for helping our team win the ball game. It's more than singing a hymn after an all-night jamboree. It is more than wearing a "Love" pin or a "Smile" button.

Being a disciple is following Jesus. It is not Jesus following us, blessing the stock market so we can hoard more possessions. It does mean we give our life, time, money, and talents to Him. We accept His orders for our life rather than ordering Him.

A journey through the Gospels indicates that being a disciple means following Jesus in a radically different way from the world. It's either Jesus or money — God or mammon. One way or another, "broad is the way . . . to destruction . . . narrow is the way . . . unto life" (Matt. 7:13,14). It's a life in the midst of God's enemies. "I send you forth as sheep in the midst of wolves" (Matt. 10:16). It's not a life of popularity. "Ye shall be hated of all men for my name's sake" (Mark 13:13).

Since God has blessed us with freedom of speech and the free-enterprise system, shouldn't we indulge and enjoy it? Many Christians justify their overindulgence by saying that God blessed them, so they should enjoy it. This reasoning beside the teachings of Jesus leaves me uncomfortable. It makes the call of Christ too cheap. Yes, we should enjoy our blessings and use them in honor of Christ, but not misuse them to satisfy our selfish desires.

With all our wealth, freedom, comfort, and self-sufficiency, how does one become a disciple of Jesus in such a rich culture? Become a hermit and hide in the mountains? Live poorly? No! This does not make you a disciple!

The first step in becoming a disciple is putting myself on God's altar and yielding my will to doing His will — saying, "God, here is my life. Use it." When I honestly yield myself to follow Christ, then my time, money, and talents become His. They go along to the altar of sacrifice to God.

On the point of time and freedom — American Christians are always busy rushing to and from, but doing what? There are many activities Christians can get involved in — good activities — yet not always are they giving God the best stewardship of their time. Being a disciple means proper use of time, letting God use it to bring hope and love to others. It may mean giving up some "good things" to do God's work. My time is not mine — but God's.

Another crucial point: Money! Some Christians say that because God gave them money they are entitled to enjoy fine cars, around-the-world vacations, and mansions with all the trimmings. They should recognize it all came from God and thank Him for it.

I don't recall reading anything like that in the Sermon on the Mount. Being a twen-

tieth-century disciple means turning your
money into Christian service. It means keeping what you need, but not measuring your
needs by the Jones-Smith rat race. It means
we remember the lost souls and hunger
pains of others as we spend our money.

Being a disciple of Jesus with money is
a challenge. A friend made a great deal of
money. However, he and his family lived
very simply, using much of their income for
the Lord's work. Now that is being a disciple!

Another test of discipleship is the use of
talents. The disciple of Jesus will open his
life to Him, permitting Jesus to make him
into a useful person in today's world. He
doesn't reserve his talents for selfish pur-
poses and useless hobbies. He permits the
Holy Spirit to make him into a person interested in the needs of others.

The disciple of Jesus will use the free
enterprise system, free-floating money, freedom of speech, and freedom of worship to
honor Jesus. He will turn these blessings
into opportunities. He will not devour them
selfishly but will use them to build God's
kingdom.

Are you willing to pay the price of
discipleship? It may be costly, but the re-
wards are eternal.

3

Confess — Repent — Grow

Testimony: "I'm so glad I took the great step and repented twenty years ago. I was an undone, vile, filthy sinner. But since that moment the evening of August 14 when I responded to Pastor Yoder's altar call, life's been different!"

I have questions about testimonies of two decades ago. They may sound good on the surface, but scratch around a bit and a different picture may come to light.

Repentance twenty years ago was a good thing, yes. But the trouble is, too often it stops there. Some people consider it repentance to say, "I'm a sinner; I accept Jesus as my Saviour," and they let it go at that, while bitterness, stubbornness, strife, self-exaltation, gossiping, and the like continue right on without any attempts at change. This is not true repentance.

True repentance is the beginning of a new way of life. It is stepping off the throne of your life and permitting Christ to occupy it in the person of the Holy Spirit. When the Holy Spirit is present in your life He will not only give you guidance on how to live, but will also convict you of sin.

Too many people seem to think, however, that once they make the initial commitment to Christ they will automatically live a sin-free life from then on. But this is not the case. So long as we are human, sin will be a problem. Thus, repentance is not a monument place. It is a starting point, a place to start running the race and go on living the repentant life.

I don't know about you, but I find repentance a continual must for myself. I can't live on my first known public confession of Jesus. I need to repent and keep on repenting. By this I don't mean to say that one must repent again and again for sins already forgiven. Sins in the past which I have already confessed are taken care of and need not be repented of again. But as the Holy Spirit convicts me day by day of those areas in my life that are not as they should be, or of sins committed, I need to repent and with the Spirit's help go on from there. That's growth!

No repentance means no growth. In the Scriptures we read:

> If we say that we have fellowship with him, and walk in darkness, we lie, and do not tell the truth .... If we say that we have no sin, we deceive ourselves, and the truth is not in us. If we confess our sins, he is faithful and just to forgive us our sins, and to cleanse us from all unrighteousness (1 John 1:6,8,9).

I've had repenting to do on attitudes, accepting other persons, and giving and accepting forgiveness, just to mention a few. I hope to grow more in Christ's likeness in these matters. That simply means I have more repenting to do. Self-improvement is not enough. When repenting stops, growth stops!

When the growth of an individual Christian stops it also hinders the growth of the Church. The proud spirit of "Look at me, I've repented!" doesn't do much to build the Church. This type of repented person puts himself in a class of his own which leaves out repenting, growing Christians, as well as those who have never attempted to confess Christ. As a result, relationships are broken. One who "doesn't need repentance anymore" isn't much help to seekers of a deeper Christian life because they can't be repenting and growing together.

For the Church to grow the spirit of repentance needs to be present, along with an attitude of humility and self-denial. The non-Christian might understand repentance better if Christians continued repenting and kept a repented spirit with meekness. Repentance needs to be shown as well as told.

The call to repentance needs to be heard loudly and clearly, not by those who boast of their repentance, but by the example of a repenting Church — which, of course, begins with the individual Christian.

"Repent ye: for the kingdom of heaven is at hand" (Matt. 3:2). Keep repenting, for it is nearer at hand than ever before.

Did you repent? Are you repenting? It may make a difference in your growth and relations with others. I prefer to still be repenting. Repentance is not a monument place but the starting point of being a repentant person, breaking free, and getting on with living.

4

Find the Right Church

A group of fellows were discussing church. Their church wasn't what they thought it should be. It was not the perfect model of perfect Christians. Since it wasn't what it ought to be they were considering joining another one.

Suppose you aren't satisfied with your present church and there is not another one around that is satisfactory, either. Then what? Should you start a new one?

Many Christians are confronted and entangled in these questions. Often, out of reaction to something in our background, we become sure our church isn't the right one. Natural inclinations are to take lessons from others who join and rejoin in search of the right church in which souls are being saved.

We do seem to have a built-in instinct to want to rally behind "where the action is." This sometimes becomes the deciding factor of which is the right church. But action and perfection are two different things. This calls for a decision of deeper values.

As for myself, I've given up on the search for a perfect church. Why? First, each group is made of about the same stuff. They are human beings. Holy as some say they are, they still show their human colors. I have been in many kinds of churches and personally listened to the problems of their members. When all the boiling is over, they still have human conflicts.

Second, the search for the perfect church would keep me occupied for life. When our life, which is like a "vapor," is over (see James 4:14), it will have been spent looking for the right church with the right people to suit our taste. Many Christians waste their lives going from church to church, causing strife and confusion as they go. There must be a more valuable search for us!

Third, the real question is missed in uptight discussions about finding a perfect church. We fail to ask how to become the perfect person to make the perfect church. This is the crucial point — becoming the right kind of person! It isn't finding the right church, but being the right kind of person in the church.

My concern now is whether or not I am becoming the right person. After all, I am a part of the church, and it is foolish for me to push all the blame of imperfection onto others. Now this is not suggesting that just any church will do. Sure, it needs to be a Bible believing, God-fearing church that teaches the Scriptures. However, the real task for each individual is to seek to become the person God meant for us to be when He created us.

Now my real task is to start being everything I think a church ought to be — better yet, to reach to become what Christ wants His Church to be. When this begins, fulfillment and purpose in life take place. Then the person becomes an optimistic, happy child of God who lives with enthusiasm for Christ. He will not be the negative person who sees everything everyone else does as doomed, and who can hardly wait for God to pour out judgment on the "sinners" around him.

There are a few things involved in becoming the right church. If I want to be a part of a church that isn't always having trouble, I'll have to be a peacemaker instead of a troublemaker. If I'm not part of the solution, I am part of the problem. If it is to be a mission church it must begin with people. It must begin with me. I must stop crying about others and go to work myself. Those who cry the loudest are often working the least. Instead of expecting others to be the model church, my challenge is to personally become that model.

Where do I go from here to be the Church? One, I center attention on being the right kind of person. I best become that person by giving up my selfish desires and giving my life to Christ and His cause. As the Bible points out, "present your bodies a living sacrifice" (Rom. 12:1). I must sacrifice my will and vow to do His will.

Two, I work to be a person through whom God's love can flow to others. My goal will be to become a giving person — giving of myself, love, compassion, talents, and blessings to others. I'll ask, "What can I give?" not "What can I get?" "It is more blessed to give than to receive" (Acts 20:35). Invest your life in persons!

Three, I'll be a Christian during conflict. Instead of blaming others for the conflict I will first check out myself, correcting any trace of the problem. Conflicts will be present. I'll accept the challenge to work through them instead of around them. I must be willing to ask, give, and receive forgiveness. I'll go sin-hunting in my own woods first.

Four, to be the Church I must practice a meaningful ministry. God doesn't call His children to a ministry of tearing down the character and ministry of their fellow man. I don't recall reading in the Bible of a ministry of criticism such as some Christians keep nursing. We must go to something constructive, discovering the true purpose of ourselves, and giving encouragement to others. Cheer up and smile! The work of Christ is the greatest and highest calling in the world.

Finally, joining the Church isn't a free ride to glory. It is a public expression of my standing with God and His people. It has a commission to keep. Keeping that commission should be my aim.

To me, being the Church means to stop searching and start building. Stop complaining and start working. Stop grumbling and start witnessing. In my experience, the work of the Church begins as I give myself to investing in persons for Christ's sake.

So instead of joining and unjoining in a search to find the perfect church, consider: "How can I become the Church? How can I become the best that God wants me to be?"

Tell God, "From this day on, I'm Yours. I'll do Your will and yield to Your Word. Make me into the Church You want." When a person starts becoming his best for God, the question of finding the right church will begin to answer itself.

5

Be Faithful Where You Are

Two teenage girls were talking, and I overheard. They lived in a beautiful farming country, but they wanted to be somewhere else, like way out West, or in Africa — just anywhere except where they were. Anywhere that would be more exciting.

We go through such a stage. We want to be something, somewhere, sometime. But usually we think of becoming that something somewhere else. "I'd like to be a missionary, but not here. A doctor, a nurse, a something — but somewhere greater than here."

We read adventure stories about people

who were in Africa or China. It may be true or it may be fiction. In any case, we are inclined to want to be like that, too. We see men with gifts of speaking and great influence on others, men of power and might. We immediately want to be like them. It has its merits and its dangers. We have a lot to learn from others, and we should. But we can't be that someone else.

God put you where you are. You didn't just happen. You were called and chosen to be there. There is a gold mine available for your life, no matter where you are. Fullness of life isn't found only in a certain place on this earth.

May we take a lesson from Mr. Allen's backyard? Mr. Allen took me on a tour through his backyard. More than half of it was garden. What a fruitful little place it was. Beans, squash, tomatoes, peaches, and figs, just to mention a few. That little spot of earth produced wonderful, delicious fresh food for his family and enough to give away to his friends. But he could have said to himself, "I must be in the right part of the country to produce food. If only I lived on a farm. No use trying here in the city." He could have given up and said the odds were against him — but he didn't. His faithfulness to that small area made it produce richly.

Did you catch the point? Why not be faithful right where you are — now? Why not take advantage of the place you are and try to become your best for God in your little corner? God put you there, so become all you can by serving Him to your fullest capacity. Then in His own good time He may say, "Well done, thou good and faithful servant: thou hast been faithful over a few things, I will make thee ruler over many things: enter thou into the joy of thy Lord" (Matt. 25:21).

Waste no time feeling sorry for yourself. Stop wishing you were someone great, somewhere else. Instead, thank God for where He put you. Then start cultivating your soil. Prepare yourself for God's call. You have been chosen by God for a ministry. You should be preparing yourself for it. The best place to start is from where you are, and there is no better time than now. Many Christians miss their ministry because they think they can't get there from where they are. But you must start from where you are to become your best for God. Waiting to give yourself to Him means days wasted that cannot be recalled and re-done. Start now to become a wholesome person for God.

But how? Take a lesson from Jesus. How did He prepare for His ministry? He was a full-grown, mature man when He began His public ministry, but until then He "increased in wisdom and stature, and in favour with God and man" (Luke 2:52). Could He be our perfect example? Like learning wisdom? We must have wisdom to be successful for God. Learn all you can from the Bible, of how men of God made good judgments in times of distress. Discover how wisdom equaled good judgment, which equaled decisions that brought hope to a hopeless people. Become wise in God's Word. There is no better way to prepare for life than to memorize God's Word and to practice it daily. I regret I didn't spend more of my younger moments memorizing the Bible. You have nothing to lose but a lot to gain by knowing the Scriptures.

Give yourself time to grow in stature. Right where you are may be the best place for that. Take Jesus' example of growing in favor with God. Make use of the spot where you live to learn God's will. Apply the Scriptures to your own life. Lose no time becoming a strong person for God and doing His will.

Grow in favor with men. Learn love toward others. Learn to appreciate and live with those nearest you. Learn kindness, patience, and compassion for those who irritate you, and forgiveness toward those who wrong you. Then you'll grow into a strong someone to be used somewhere.

Remember David? He watched sheep by himself. He learned faith and trust where he was, out by himself in fellowship with God. His faith and trust became so great that he was used by God to slay a giant and save a nation.

Your life is somewhat like Mr. Allen's backyard. There is a great potential there. So what are you going to do about yourself where you are? You could sow your life full of self-pity, envy, jealousy, anger, and fear. Or you could yield yourself totally to God and permit His Spirit to fill your life with love, joy, peace, compassion, kindness, and forgiveness. That would produce so much fruit that others would benefit from it. You could have the joy of giving a listening ear and an understanding heart in caring for others. But, of course, you hold the seeds in your control, and you'll have to decide what seeds you sow, good or bad, fruit or weeds. It's up to you.

To be your best tomorrow, become your best today. Start planting your garden of life. Fill your yard with the fruit of God's Spirit so you'll be prepared to go some-where, anywhere, when He calls you to the ministry He already has for you. That's living!

6

Challenge Your Own Convictions

You probably wouldn't believe it, but the people you like least may be running your life. They may be molding your thinking and developing your convictions. "Never!" you say. Would you mind taking a test to see if this is true?

Let's consider the persons or organizations you like the least. There are things about them you hate, right? So to be sure you don't become like them you avoid doing things the same way they do. You react to them by being careful not to follow their style of life.

If the above situation fits you, then

your enemy is developing your life. You aren't free to follow honest convictions. You are living by reaction instead of conviction.

Here is a reactionist story: There were some people who couldn't get along in their church. Their word wasn't the final word so they reacted and left. Now they were on their own, with no church telling them what was right and what was wrong. So what should they do? They couldn't do things the way they did before — they must believe differently to win their case. If they baptized, held communion, went by a name, or met in a church, they would be like the church they left. So they found "scriptural" ways to be different. No communion, no name, no meetinghouse, just to mention a few things. In a real way, the church they left was running their lives. Their reactions to the church were molding their beliefs. While the life of the church they despised went on, their own bitterness made them into contemptible, stubborn, more-enlightened-than-thou people. They lived their lives in reaction to their "enemies," rather than in honest truth learned from God's Word.

Aren't we much like that sometimes? Evangelistic efforts may be the result of reaction rather than conviction.

Take another example: Some people lost faith in their brotherhood and charged it with not obeying the Great Commission. They left in the name of evangelism and joined another church to live out their convictions. What happened? They were active and faithful — for a while — but now it's all over and they have settled down to routine worldly living. Their evangelism "convictions" are history. Was it conviction, or could it have been a reaction to something, the reaction taking shape in being "for" evangelism?

Reactions wear off. Convictions from the Word of God move to action and faithfulness through love.

There are people who have gone to extremes on being "modest" and not conforming to the world's dress standards. Talk about nonconformity, they had it! (But they still needed to be transformed.) On the other side of the issue, Christians have disregarded all discipline, and have accepted the latest thing in designs from the fashion world. Was that following honest convictions or were reactions determining their attitudes?

A friend may overcorrect his child. You react and under-discipline yours.

Your neighbor goes to the doctor too often to suit your taste, so you react and don't go at all.

People are mistreated because of their race. Others react and go to extremes to correct it. They may marry someone of another race just to prove a point. Or, we see violence from civil rights demands, and we react by saying if that is the way they are going to be, let them go back to Africa.

One woman is a sloppy housekeeper. Another woman reacts and won't let her family "live" because it clutters up the house.

So, you see, convictions may be formed from reactions. The person you fell out with may become the governing influence in your life.

The angry crowd that cried, "Crucify!" didn't ask for the release of Barabbas because they loved him. Rather, they asked for the release of one they didn't really want set free because they hated Jesus.

Convictions can be formed from hatred. When love and respect are lost, hatred comes in. Reactions move to stated convictions.

When we react to people negatively we close them out of our lives. We close out the possibility of learning and growing. Sometimes God uses our least loved ones to lead us through a growing experience.

When one closes people out of his life by reaction he is robbing his own life. Just because we are Christians doesn't give us all the answers to everything. Reacting to another makes life less worthwhile for both of you. Responding with deep-seated Bible convictions in the Jesus way of life and love will add enthusiasm to your life.

What kind of person will have convictions to follow Christ's style of life? He will love God, be committed to Him, and be led by the Holy Spirit with resulting fruits. God's Word is his guide. Issues are faced and dealt with in the light of God's Word. He can listen to another's views and grow, yet not be swayed from the truth. In 2 Timothy 2:15 and 16 we read, "Study to shew thyself approved unto God, a workman that needeth not to be ashamed, rightly dividing the word of truth. But shun profane and vain babblings: for they will increase unto more ungodliness."

Challenge your convictions. Discover whether you are living on convictions or reactions. Check on your life by these questions: Do you love God with all your heart? Do you love your fellowmen as yourself? Do you esteem the other person better than yourself? Do you stay with the issue and not attack the other person's character? Do you stay free from bitter attitudes? If your answers are no, reactions may be running — and ruining — your life!

7

Give Yourself

"Please come to the Memorial Church next Sunday for the dedication of the new church library. The Most Reverend will recite a prayer, followed by a review of church history presented by the president of the Board of Deacons. The Hallelujah Singers will do a rendition, with the overseeing bishop pronouncing the benediction. Please take thirty minutes of your time for this important dedication."

Dedicate to God a new church library? Gladly! But when it comes to dedicating our lives — ourselves — often it's a different story.

We gladly give God a building, an organ, or maybe even some of our money. It makes us feel so good and righteous inside. But, I wonder, are buildings and things really what God wants? I don't recall reading in the Scriptures that we are to present *things* to God for a living sacrifice. They are already His. God does call for people to "present your bodies a living sacrifice, holy, acceptable unto God" (Rom. 12:1).

That is the dedication God wants. He wants man to dedicate himself. Then God will live in man's spirit. God will use that person to carry on His will and to express His love through that person to others. His love does not flow through things. It flows through those who dedicate themselves to Him.

Am I saying we shouldn't dedicate things to God? No! I'm saying dedicate yourself first — without reservation of things. When you go to the dedication altar, your things, time, money, and life will go along. When God gets you, you yield Him your things. They then become tools for you to use to do His will.

Do I say it is wrong to dedicate a church building? Not really. It should happen *only* if the people are dedicated to God. For people who are not dedicated to give Him a building is mockery! If a church building is dedicated, there should first be an examination of the dedication of the people. God can't use a building if His Spirit doesn't dwell in the people.

Dedication of things may be an escape from dedication of self. Man doesn't mind attending a dedication service of something if he can go on with his own interests after the benediction. We'll give if we don't need to become personally involved. "God, here is fifty dollars, but I don't have time to pray. I'll give money, but not a vital prayer period. I'll give a machine, but don't involve me in service. I'll bring my child to the altar, but I don't have time to be a parent. I'll give an organ, but don't expect sanctified living (a life set apart for God). Here is a guitar for You, God, but I can't make it on Christian behavior. God, here are a lot of things, but I'll pass when it comes to steadfastness and holiness." Yes, dedication of things may only be an escape from the dedication God really wants. *He wants you!*

Man is naturally selfish. He wants to do things for himself. God's people, Israel, were continually using escapes from dedication, obedience, and holiness. They offered many things to gods, even their own babies! These dedications only led to their downfall and destruction. The same spirit is still in man today. He is willing to give things at the expense of himself.

God wants dedication of persons —

submission and obedience to His Word, a life set apart for His cause. To put it another way: His Spirit wants to move into our spirit at our invitation, then control us, fill us, and use us in His service so that we'll be walking in the Spirit, doing His will, and working in His kingdom.

God has a kingdom, a program, and a plan for the future. Abraham, Isaiah, David, Paul, and Peter were men used in shaping the history of God's program. These men dedicated their lives to God. Their dedication to God was of utmost importance. God has a place for you to fit into His plan. To fit in and function you must turn yourself in to Him through dedication. He then can use you in His program.

Don't try to buy God short by giving Him things instead of yourself. Break free from phony dedications. Give Him yourself.

8

Be Sure Your Pilot Knows How to Fly

Suppose you have just bought a ticket for a flight on a 747 jumbo jet. As you ascend the steps to board your pilot greets you at the door with a "Welcome aboard!"

"I've never flown a plane before in my life," he explains, "but don't worry, I know all the tricks, all the answers. I've read books on how to fly, and I have the know-how. You have nothing to worry about! May I have your ticket, please?"

If you were faced with a situation such as that, would you go?

I don't know about you, but for me life is too precious to chance it on an inexperienced pilot. Yet some people run their lives like that. They reject the experienced counsel of people who have been over the rough spots and who have reached a greater level of spiritual growth. Instead they accept the advice of someone who has never even gotten off the runway spiritually.

"Premarital sex is okay," a friend might say. "Everybody's doing it. Don't be such an old fogey." Or, "Why not cheat on your income tax? A fellow needs all the help he can get. Besides, what are a few dollars to the government, anyway?" So you grab his ticket and fly your life on his inexperienced advice.

You try to cross out what the people God put in charge of your life have been telling you. You cross out advice from those who have been through the tough spots in life. You ignore those who have been over the route before and know where the air pockets are that might knock you out of line with God. Yes, many choose to follow the advice of inexperienced people.

When I want to get through a tough spot in life I ask someone who has been over the way before me. He talks in a language I understand. He talks reality, not chapter 3 of a certain book. Neither do I ask a man who never faces tough spots, because he wouldn't know how to get through.

There are people who have a habit of running for other ground as soon as they get in a pinch. When trouble strikes, they are gone. They bypass the issue, push the sin undercover, and head out, leaving a sticky situation behind in which others get hung up. And usually they have a lot of free advice to give as they go. Caution! Advice from a man who moves out when trials of life move in may be hazardous to your spiritual health.

Strange as it may seem, I find myself putting my trust in those who conquer and overcome instead of running. When all the dust has settled and the smoke has cleared, I'd ask the remaining man on the field, "How did you do it?"

You wouldn't take your typewriter to your five-year-old brother or eighty-year-old grandmother for repair. You would take it to a man who has repaired typewriters before and knows his stuff. If you wouldn't gamble on a typewriter, why gamble on life? Your life is a priceless possession. Be cautious from whom you take directions.

I've taken advice from those who weren't over the road before me but were seeking the way with me. We advised each other. Sometimes it paid off; sometimes it cost a price. It was a chance. The better advice comes from those who have gone ahead and know the way.

Don't expect wrong ideas and temptations always to come wrapped up in a devil's suit. As John Gimenez points out, it was his best friend who started him on dope. A Christian's downfall may very well come from the influence of a close but immature friend who advises before he knows all the facts.

King Rehoboam sought counsel from the older men. They advised him. He rejected their advice and sought counsel from the young men with whom he had grown up. The king took the advice of his peers. Because he accepted the wrong advice, the people chose to desert him, and the kingdom was divided (2 Chron. 10).

Or how about Samson? He accepted the wrong way and "the Lord was departed from him" (Judg. 16:20). The prodigal son took his own inexperienced advice, and life turned into a failure. On the other hand, Joseph's faithfulness and submission showed his master "that the Lord was with him" (Gen. 39:3). His submission saved his people from famine. Timothy gave heed to those who walked before him (2 Tim. 1:1-5). Paul commended him for it. He didn't need to be sorry about it. He saved himself a lot of trouble.

Proverbs 13:10 tells us, "With the well

advised is wisdom." Take time to consider the counsel of the voices who have experienced living before you. Don't let good advice drop out of reach. It's a choice with which you may want to stay in touch.

The best guide and example for life is Jesus Christ. But we are all influenced by those around us. So be careful whose advice you follow. Be sure your pilot knows how to fly!

9

Follow God, Not "Sarah"

"God is leading us to another place," the pastor of a large congregation assured his members. On the surface this appeared to be true, but as various members of the congregation visited the pastor's home to give their farewells, they began to have their doubts.

Repeatedly in their conversations with the pastor and his family a character named Sarah came up for discussion. It began to be evident that "Sarah" was the irritation — and the real reason the pastor and family were leaving. But to polish over the situation they called it "God's leading."

Sometimes Christians are being moved by a "Sarah" in their lives. To blanket it over they declare that God led them. "God led me," they say, or, "I feel it is God's will." They give no concrete evidence, only feelings.

At times I feel strongly that God is leading, but later I see I was wrong. Sometimes I don't feel like He is leading at all, and it proves to be that He was. Feelings alone cannot be trusted. Following feelings can cause disappointments later.

Christians may be tempted by things and practices that do not agree with Scripture. Since they desire them, they may try to make themselves feel it would be all right. After they have indulged they declare they feel it was God's will — with feelings being the only evidence. All too often the phrase "It is God's will" is used to justify our own lusts and desires.

The phrase "God led me" is being used by some to shove their way through any sin in which they wish to indulge. For example, I know of a lady who was "led" to divorce her husband; another was "led" by a special revelation to marry a divorced man.

You can persuade yourself to accept sinful living if this is your desire. But it is a dangerous desire. If you insist on your way of thinking God will give you up to "do your own thing." It happened to the Romans. They wanted their own way. "Because men refuse to keep in mind the true knowledge about God, he has given them over to corrupted minds, so that they do the things that they should not" (Rom. 1:28;TEV). Warning! Taking your own way is dangerous!

A lot of Christians get their "God leading" directions because some "Sarah" may be pushing. They don't get their own way in a given situation. They are displeased. They linger in thought on the humiliation of having to "give in." Soon the issue is buried in character-attacking and a "Sarah" develops from it. A final alternative is taken to honest submission. They leave, like a child in a game who can't have his own way. Appearing with supposedly clean hands and an innocent look, they make God look like the failure, pushing the blame onto Him with their smoothing-over remark: "God led us to leave."

If there is a person-to-person conflict, the maturing Christian will do his part to resolve it. The immature Christian will harbor thoughts of how wrong this terrible person is, and how right he himself is. He thinks of getting back at the other person by cutting off communications and relationships. If that doesn't satisfy his ego, he moves out. Instead of confessing that he is running from his "Sarah," he shifts his inconsistencies onto God, boasting that God led him.

Man either accepts the blame for his failures or shifts it onto another. We make God appear to be the failure by refusing to accept our responsibilities. To gain spiritual esteem from others we say, "God led us." I get a feeling that some Christians who herald, "God led me," should be confessing offenses instead. Then God could lead!

The term "God led me" is sometimes used as a means of slapping another brother and proving him wrong. If a person is challenged on an issue in his life that is not scriptural, the challenger may be cut off by a slap back: "God led me." Now what can one say to that?

I detest the attitude of the Christian who insists on his own way, then slaps back with "It's God's will," though he has no concrete evidence on which to base this statement.

May I urge that we be very careful how "Sarahs" push us around? Don't let one who disagrees with you push you into harboring ill feelings toward him or another person. If that happens, that person is your "Sarah," and you have been pushed. If those feelings continue you may be pushed right out of the Kingdom!

Perhaps there is an issue at church on which you disagree with another's viewpoint. You desire God's leading on the issue, but if you aren't careful some "Sarah" will push you into an "I'm dead right" position. It happens so cunningly. You declare it was God who led you. A person can afford to be wrong on an issue — that can be corrected. But your spiritual life cannot afford to permit any disagreeing "Sarah" to push you into bitter attitudes toward anyone. That is courting spiritual suicide.

Abraham, the hero of faith, was pushed by his "Sarah" to sidestep God's leading for his life. She lost faith in God's promises and took it upon herself to help Him out. She talked Abraham into having a child with their maid. Ishmael was born because of her pushing and there has been trouble ever since between the kinfolks — the Jews and the Arabs (Gen. 16).

Our "Sarahs" may be our brothers. Some are right. Some are wrong. We can use their pushing in our lives to soar us to a higher spiritual level. It is our response that will lift us or bury us!

Am I saying God doesn't lead men today? No! God does lead men today. He began at creation and He will lead so long as men follow Him. I know saints who are being led by God — but humbly, sincerely, and respectfully. What I am saying is that it is a shame and a dishonor to God to claim that He led when it was only our own selfish desires we followed. It is a disgrace to His image and reputation!

How can we determine whether or not God is leading us? Here are several suggestions that may be starters to discovering God's will:

One — openly and honestly ask God to show you His will. His Word says, "Call unto me, and I will answer thee, and shew thee great and mighty things, which thou knowest not" (Jer. 33:3).

After asking, search for signals in the Bible, the message of God's will for His people. If the action contradicts Christian behavior as taught in the Bible, then rest assured God is not leading. The Holy Spirit can reveal God's will to you as you pray, search His Word, and trust God's promises.

Two — examine the contemplated action under the microscope of 1 Corinthians 13. Would the action be out of love for others? Would it be for the good of others? Or would it be to satisfy a vengeful ego, or to show another person he is wrong? The Love Chapter states "Love does not keep a record of wrongs" (1 Cor. 13:5;TEV). God's will is easier to discover if our attitudes are spiritually healthy and loving toward all people.

Three — sift the action through the Golden Rule. "Therefore do all things whatsoever ye would that men should do to you, do ye even so to them" (Matt. 7:12). If the action or move is something you wouldn't want others to do to you, then be cautious — it probably isn't God leading. Perhaps resentment may be pushing.

Four — sterilize the action through the oven of forgiveness. If the action is a move to satisfy a past grudge toward another person, then forgiveness needs to take place in order to receive the clearest directions from God.

Five — watch for open and closed doors. At times God leads through opportunities, or "open doors." Other times He reveals His will by closing doors. In seeking God's will believers should be careful not to force doors open when God has closed them.

Finally — be open to counsel from others. Be willing to listen to what God may be telling you through fellow believers. God often uses others to help us determine His will. He may even send His counsel through those persons we'd rather not hear from. It doesn't always come from those we usually agree with.

Let me urge that we use the term "God led me" cautiously, meekly, and humbly.

Our selfish desires must not dishonor His name!

As you move and act, check carefully — is the idea from God, or only an ill attitude you developed from some "Sarah" in your life? Following God's leading is a step forward with living.

10

Forget It?
No, Forgive It!

Ouch! There went the end of my finger. My hand slipped from the narrow strip of paneling right onto the knives of the jointer. With blood squirting from the wound, I call for help. My co-worker soon has me in the hospital emergency room. I'm in pain and not exactly rejoicing that my nail and part of the finger are ground to shavings. At a time when a bit of sympathy would feel good, a person close to me comes in and makes a cutting remark.

That was years ago. Did I forget? My finger is ugly — sometimes painful. It gets cold. My eyes see it clearly (maybe 490 times a day). The pain, the cold, the ugly finger, the relived feeling of the grinding knives mean the remembered pain of the remark. Does that mean I haven't forgiven? Must one forget to forgive?

"Forgive and forget" we've been saying for years. I challenge that! Forgetting is not forgiving. Forgiving is bearing the hurt and the price of the hurt and letting the guilty go free. Jesus bore the hurt to pay the price of sin so that we may go free. That's forgiveness.

To say "forgive and forget" is asking the impossible. I haven't forgotten the hurt that accompanied my wounded finger. If I could forget it, I wouldn't need to forgive it.

Remember the standard Sunday school question on forgiveness: "Did you forgive if you didn't forget?" Forgiving has a price with it that is remembered. The peace, joy, and release of forgiving are not soon forgotten, either, but may be cherished for years. A forgiven matter cost and hurt the one who forgave. Costs and hurts aren't soon forgotten. If you are trying to forget it, chances are it hasn't been forgiven.

Forgetting pulls other problems into focus. First, forgetting does happen — forgetting to forgive. The hurt is swept undercover, and we figure if it is forgotten it is forgiven. Not so! If it is forgiven it may be remembered, because forgiven persons become special brothers who love and appreciate each other. Honest forgiveness draws people together. I owe the ones who forgave me deep respect, love, and brotherhood, which comes from knowing I'm set free. You become a precious brother because you have forgiven me — not because you've forgotten me.

Second problem: forgetting also forgets the person. We prefer to dismiss the wrong deed. In so doing we dismiss the person, too. Forgetting forgets to rebuild friendship and brotherhood. My human nature prefers to forget and pretend my past isn't there. I can't forget — but I can forgive! In forgiving I want to include both the offender and the offended in my Christian fellowship.

Demanding that a hurting brother forget may simply prevent him from forgiving. Drop the notion of forgetting. Help him forgive. The more he tries to forget, the better he remembers. He needs love and understanding that will help him let the person who wronged him go free. He needs help to bear the cost and pain of granting release. He needs encouragement to step to new freedom himself.

Third problem: forgetting forgets to love. Trying to forget the hurt we can't forget anyway robs us of brotherly love. We love Christ because He forgave. Likewise, we love each other because of forgiveness given and received. I love you more deeply because you forgave me. When we forget the hurt, we forget to love.

Paul speaks of "forgetting those things which are behind, and reaching forth unto those things which are before" (Phil. 3:13). This is a text sometimes used to prove one ought to "forgive and forget." That is out of context. As I read the entire chapter I see no broken personal relationship that is being forgiven and then forgotten. Rather, Paul is forgetting what more believers ought to forget. He remembers the old, ungodly, selfish person that he was. Now that he is in Christ he is forgetting to be the old person he once was. He has opened his life to Christ so fully that he is forgetting to sin. As one person put it in today's experience, "I never had to give up drinking, I just didn't want it anymore." Because of Christ's Spirit in you, and your commitment to Him, press forward in His service and you'll forget to sin. Forget? Yes, forget to indulge in sin. I think it is unfair to throw this Scripture at a hurting brother and say, "Paul forgot!" We must help him move forward so the hurt can begin healing. Then if he forgets — that's wonderful!

This does not mean it is right to keep reminding and using a forgiven deed against another. It is wrong to bump the bruise to make it hurt or to salt the hurt to make it burn. These actions may mean forgiveness hasn't happened yet on your part.

Another angle of forgiveness comes from Peter's question: "How oft shall my brother sin against me, and I forgive him? till seven times?" Jesus' answer — 490 times (Matt. 18:21,22).

How could anyone sin against me 490 times a day and need forgiveness? That means he would have to sin every three minutes twenty-four hours a day. That calls for a continually forgiving spirit. No one sins against you that often. But you may need to forgive that much.

A wrongdoing inflicting deep hurt isn't forgiven and then forgotten in a moment. The pain of hurt and resentment hits way down deep inside the very heart of one's nerve center. The sight of things, recollection of events, remarks of others — all these keep reminding you that you've been wronged. So forgive — 490 times a day if necessary. Forgive 490 times if the deep temptation and pain of retaliation returns that often. Forgiveness continues as often as the reminder of the deed and hurt return.

Maybe we could best forgive if we celebrated forgiveness. Since my brother forgave, why not enjoy his fellowship by dining together? Something good happened. A hurt began healing; broken relationships are being repaired; a wrong is repented — that is worth rejoicing about.

From the parable of the prodigal son I understand that forgiveness called for the fatted calf of rejoicing — not a forgetting session. Christ wants us to remember that He forgave. Christians remember it by the symbol called communion. It reminds us that Jesus paid the price; He set us free. He forgave. "Do this in remembrance of Me" (Luke 22:19).

Becoming a Christian is receiving Christ's forgiveness. Receiving and giving forgiveness makes a Christian brotherhood. Sharing the good news of forgiveness is the message of God's forgiven people. Forgiveness is a vital key to being the Church and getting on with living. It deserves a good slice of our attention in order to be God's people.

My finger gets cold. Uncomfortable. Sometimes it hurts. Sometimes I'm tempted to become bitter about the remarks these pains bring to memory. What can I do? Forget? No! I can keep on forgiving as often as the hurt gives a signal to forgive again. I think that is what forgiving might be. What do you think?

Forget it? No! Remember to forgive it! Then get on with living!

11

Put the Put-Down on Pride

As a boy in school, I argued for Chevys. Several of us boys counted cars as they went by. I spotted Chevys and cheered when more Chevys passed by than Fords. One day I saw a car approaching that looked like a Chevy. I said, "Chevy." My friend said, "Oldsmobile." There was an argument. As it got closer I knew I was wrong. But — own up to being wrong? The car passed by, as *Olds* as could be. I insisted it was a Chevy. Why? My pride didn't want to back off.

That was in my boyhood days. I'm not rid of the problem yet — as when a Christian brother installed a tissue paper oil cleaner on his engine. He suggested that I might want one, too. My first reaction — not I, a tissue paper oil cleaner at such a price! Before really looking at the facts I bucked it and refused.

Why refuse to at least hear the facts? To give in would have meant for me to step down and look up to him in recognition that he had something better. You see, we generally have the best tractor, the best machine, and the best bargain. But I kept seeing his clean oil from his ten-cent filter change. Now I'm a satisfied user, too. Pride was the problem.

Another case was a discussion with an elderly man about eternal punishment. He said there was no such thing. I said there was. Being fresh from the country, I was not about to change this city man's mind. He didn't budge. I still think I was right, but why insist on the last word? Right or wrong, we want the last word. So there I was, right in my belief, but too proud to let him have the last word. Perhaps the conversation would have been more effective if he had had the last words at my will, and I had let the Holy Spirit do the work.

Pride isn't always expressed like a peacock. It has more subtle ways. It comes in a more humble-looking shell. Pride puts me first. It prevents confession of being wrong.

It prevents listening to others and keeps the other person from being heard. It kills brotherhood and keeps our brother at arm's length. No wonder the Bible says, "Pride, do I hate" (Prov. 8:13).

If it wasn't for my pride I could confess my wrong and go free. I could be released from my guilt and have peace with my fellow believers. That would give me freedom to release the gift God has given me. I'd be free to move on in a God-directed ministry. I'd be free to go on encouraging the believers in faith, free to start building the Church. I could say, "Brother, I was wrong," and go on enjoying the richest that life has to offer.

If it wasn't for pride we might prevent a church split. We might junk our turtle shells, come out, and own up to being part of the conflict. That would give freedom to become a healer. But so long as pride keeps sin tucked under the shell, the problem will exist. A lot of splinter churches are started because of pride. No one wants to say, "I was wrong, I hurt you, I have sinned." Pride won't let us do that. Rather than confess, we split.

If it wasn't for pride I could smile, be happy, and enjoy people. The sight of me wouldn't turn the other person's nerves into a knot. I'm being threatened by those better than I. I fear them. Pride prevents rejoicing about the good of others. Pride says, "I'll never own one of those things like yours, go to your doctor, shop at you store, or be caught in your church."

If it wasn't for pride I could be a more effective soul winner. People could see the other face I'm hiding and find out what I really am. It would mean owning up that I am a sinner, not trusting any good work to merit eternal life. It means confessing that I am a Christian by virtue of God's unmerited love and forgiveness. That is what makes me a saint.

Pride takes people to hell. If it wasn't for pride, people would bow to Jesus and confess Him as Lord of their life. But that means confessing yourself a failure, owning up to being insufficient, bowing out to self.

Pride is destructive. "Pride goeth before destruction" (Prov. 16:18). The person who boasts about himself destroys the possibility of becoming his best for God. But we usually show our pride in a more humble wrapper. It is just as destructive — like no matter what the facts are, I'm still right — or showing the other person up wrong in order to appear to be right. Few of us would say, "Look, I was right." But we barely hesitate to say he was wrong. That is destructive pride in a self-made wrapper.

Pride asks us to save our life and our image. Jesus said, "Whosoever will save his life shall lose it; but whosoever shall lose his life for my sake and the gospel's, the same shall save it" (Mark 8:35). To find myself, I must release myself in Christ. I must give myself the opportunity to be wrong, to be vulnerable, to give and accept forgiveness. When I dethrone self and enthrone Christ it gives release from pride. Then I'm free to become one of His people living in joy, free to become what He wants me to be.

The good news is that pride is not a hopeless case. When the Lord Jesus is enthroned to rule a person's life, Christ begins a renewing work in that person's life. When we admit we can't handle our pride, and call for His help, He answers. The Bible says, "Now the God of peace, that brought again from the dead our Lord Jesus .... Make you perfect in every good work to do his will, working in you that which is wellpleasing in his sight, through Jesus Christ" (Heb. 13:20,21). That is it! The God who raised Jesus from the dead wants to raise you to new life. He wants to change you from pride to loving, caring meekness.

How does this happen? I can't do it myself. Therefore, I must be honest with God and own up to that fact. Then, seeking His help, I will trust and believe His promise that He will work it out in me and make me "perfect in every good work to do his will," so I can do "that which is wellpleasing in his sight, through Jesus Christ." Turn yourself over to Him, and trust Him to do the good work. When we believe and trust His promise, He will do it.

Pride is from the spirit of the world. "The pride of life is not of the Father, but is of the world" (1 John 2:16). The unsaved world sets up a standard to reach for, a way of life that glorifies the person.

Pride says follow to keep your image. Christ says, "Lose yourself in Me."

Pride makes a Chevy out of an Olds. Pride can't hear his brother and demands the last word. Think of the dynamic Christian I might become if it wasn't for my pride.

Pride prevents confession. It is a killer of brotherhood, the enlarger of hell. It's a human problem. It's a problem Christ wants lost in Him. It's a problem that prevents a person from getting on with the best of living.

12

Don't Live by the Advertisements

"We just want to make you happy," the car dealer says. He's convinced you that your presently owned automobile is hopelessly lacking in all the necessary conveniences, and you just *must* buy that new model in his showroom in order to retain your self-respect.

"Brand A is most effective," one advertiser says. "Brand B is more convenient, saves time and work," claims another. "You'll be happier with Brand C," says still another.

And so it goes as advertisers debate and compete in an attempt to get us to buy their products — whether we really need them or not.

Are you letting yourself be convinced, as the advertisers seem to indicate, that it's essential to your happiness, peace of mind, and self-respect to own the most up-to-date car, the newest style of clothes, or the latest gadgets?

Are you living by the advertisements?

The following are some scriptural guidelines to help us draw our spending into a more Christian perspective.

First: "Seek ye first the kingdom of God, and his righteousness; and all these things [the necessary things] shall be added unto you" (Matt. 6:33).

Practice Kingdom buying. Does what you are buying have anything to do with God's kingdom? Is the spending supplying a need or is it only to satisfy your personal ego? Before you buy, consider God. Put Him first.

Second: "Love God with all your heart, mind, and soul" (Matt. 22:37). Can you imagine what would happen if the Church put her time, energy, and money to work for Christ because of love for Him? Just think what kind of a community that would be!

But we are drunk with affluence! Addiction to the world and its things is Satan's stronghold in America. If Christians would love Christ with all their hearts, then He would cast out the world demons that grip us.

Third: Learn contentment. Paul said, "I have learned . . . to be content" (Phil. 4:11). His contentment didn't come from things, but from a personal faith in Christ. While the world is striving for more wealth to buy the best comforts, to enjoy the most pleasure, we need contentment.

The Christian should learn to trust in God to supply his needs. His energy should be channeled into service for Christ rather than being expended to gain more materially.

North American Christians become discontent after comparing themselves with society. If we must compare, then let's compare our luxuries with that on which the South American barely exists. Learn to be content with less.

Fourth: Keep the focus heavenward, "from whence also we look for the Saviour" (Phil. 3:20). Our way of life is from heaven. We are citizens of heaven. We would do well to pay more attention to our citizenship and less to temporal things.

Differences which divide us are often caused by our discontentment because of another's wealth. Our conversation centers too much on who is making the cash and how. The moneymaker is projected as the real man, while the earthly poorer but spiritually rich individual is made to look like a welfare tagalong. This breeds discontentment and breaks down the equality of brotherhood in Christ.

To be a disciple means giving Jesus our undivided loyalty. He must be our way of life. No divided attention on time, money, and possessions. No using Him just as a first class ticket to heaven. He wants all of you.

The enemy of Jesus wants to make us uncomfortable so we will give him the attention and loyalty which belong to Jesus alone. Then, instead of showing loyalty to Christ, we make "things" our god. Instead of trusting, we watch the stock market. Instead of being content with the basic needs of life, we want a little more.

But there is more to life than the endless struggle to obtain material things. Real living is found in yielding to Christ and serving Him with all your heart, mind, and strength.

I refuse to let the advertisers tell me when I need a new car. When my present car doesn't serve me anymore, then I'll start looking for what I need. I don't want them messing with my wardrobe. When my shoes wear out, then I'll buy others. I'll look for something practical, comfortable, and decent to wear in serving Jesus. After all, I'm dressing in His honor.

I refuse to spend my God-entrusted money because some style designers decide heels should be higher and trouser legs flared. That is the trick of the system — to make you feel out of tune with the world, unhappy, uncomfortable, and discontented, until you spend to "fit in."

My life is not dedicated to keeping the system going but to Jesus, who has led me into a freedom from the world system. The simple life-style I enjoy is not a burden but a freedom — freedom from the monthly payments for gadgets. It gives me more freedom to move forward with God's work and the important things in life.

Don't let the advertisers run your life. Be content in Christ, doing that which pleases Him! Let Him rearrange your values. Then you can be set free from the god of temporal things and be free to get on with real living!

13

Stop Fussing and Build Something!

The children are on the living room floor, toys scattered, fussing at each other. You must have told them a dozen times to be more quiet. They are wrecking your nerves as well as the living room. "Please, children, stop fussing! Take your blocks and build something. A house, a barn, a bridge, anything — just build something!"

Children are such lovely little people when they play constructively without scrapping. It is a great pleasure to watch a child use his imagination in building things. It is fascinating to watch children as they are playing and building and not fussing. But when they stray from building to fussing, the good advice for them is to "stop fussing and build something."

That may be good advice for us as God's children, too. Stop fussing and build something.

Many Christians I know aren't building; they are fussing — complaining about what is wrong with everyone else. As sure as the sun rises they can find something wrong with the preacher, the church, the school, the neighbor, the government, and national and international affairs. The youth have "gone to the dogs," the church is "off beam," and the world is "in the last step of its last leg."

Perhaps so. There may be truth behind the accusations. But that does not call for Christians to start criticizing, complaining, and knocking over structures — persons or organizations — that may already be weak. Rather, Christians should be building solid foundations — foundations of faith in God. The happy Christians I know are building something.

Each of us should be involved in building a healing ministry. Work on building the church, a better community, a better world. That would be far better than all the complaining you could do in your entire lifetime! When the complainer and the critic reach their sunsets, what will they have to show for their life's ministry? Children — children of God — stop fussing and build something!

I've been around a few years. I've done some fussing myself. But when the fussing was finished I didn't feel much better. Sometimes I felt worse. And the problem was still there.

I have complained about rotten literature on the public market, but it didn't help much. Now, the ministry of placing good books on the public market does more good than all the complaining I could ever do. It is a positive ministry that is bringing blessings to many people. It is building the Church and a better world.

The Christian needs to examine himself and ask, "Am I building? Am I allowing God to use me to build His church?" There is some kind of building for everyone to do!

We are in a destructive world. Christians need to repent of this destructiveness and become "light" and "salt." After listening to the gloomy reports of some Christians, I almost feel like pulling my own hair. According to them it is all darkness with little hope.

The rest of your life is ahead of you. You can choose to be a builder or a complainer. You can evaluate what you would like to become, and what God would like for you to be. Then you must start disciplining yourself to become a builder with God.

Resolve for one week not to complain about anyone or anything. If you catch yourself violating your resolution, stop — stop there! Replace the remark with something that encourages and builds. Then, after testing yourself in this manner for one week, take a review. Discover if that isn't really the kind of person you would like to be. If it is, keep disciplining yourself, with God's help, to become that kind of person.

God's people should give encouragement, hope, love, and comfort, as did Paul:

> You know that we treated each one of you just as a father treats his own children. We encouraged you, we comforted you, and we kept urging you to live the kind of life that pleases God, who calls you to share his own Kingdom and glory (1 Thess. 2:11,12;TEV).

These are the characteristics we need to develop in our daily lives. The people we meet will receive encouragement rather than an atmosphere of despair and gloom. Then they, too, will want to know the Saviour we know.

God's people complained long ago: "And when the people complained, it displeased the Lord" (Num. 11:1). Complaining was a result of their selfish desires. They wanted to partake of the old life. So they complained.

Complaining brings discouragement. Discouragement allows Satan to fill our minds with evil ideas. These ideas often lead to sinful acts to fulfill our selfish lusts and egos. Thus, complaining is a thing we must weed out! Paul tells Christians not to complain as some of the Israelites did and were destroyed by the Angel of Death (1 Cor. 10:10).

Why not transfer our grumbling energy into building? There are sick people to be visited. Don't complain about others not visiting them — go yourself! There are people to be won for Jesus. Don't waste your breath grumbling because your church isn't winning souls — transfer that energy into winning souls yourself and in showing others how. You are a part of the church, so build!

Please don't raise a storm and split a church because others aren't winning souls. After that you won't be an effective witness, either. Don't grumble because love isn't being shown. Show love yourself. Then others may catch on.

Replace malice with love, bitterness with kindness, criticism with encouragement, and faultfinding with praise. "Do everything without complaining or arguing" (Phil. 2:14;TEV). Give comfort and encouragement and keep on urging people to live for God.

To do this you need a deep commitment to Christ — you need to yield to the Holy Spirit's shaping you into obedience to God's Word. You need a will that is yielded to do God's will. It means stripping off selfish ego, loving God with all your heart, and telling Him to take over your life.

We can become builders for God if we allow Him to do the building through us. God gave you one life. You can choose to use it to build or to tear down. Children! Children of God! Stop fussing and build something!

14

Help Stop the Tragic Devaluation

In the past years the value of the dollar has become less and less. But even though the dollar has been devalued, to some it is still worth more than the life of a human being.

For example: An old lady walks down the street. A mugger knocks the life out of her to gain access to some dollars in her purse. Her life is cheap.

What's in the garbage cans? Humans. People. Heads, arms, legs, and feet. It's called abortion. Life has become so cheap and devalued, according to a report by Americans Against Abortion, that one and a half million lives will be taken from people in one year's time here in America.

These lives will be taken from persons by pulling the bodies apart by suction. Or by salt poisoning and scalding the life out of them. Or by simply letting the unborn persons lie on a table (or in a trash can) squirming, wiggling, and gasping for breath until life is gone. Lust, sex, selfishness, and irresponsibility are valued higher than the lives of one and a half million persons.

The taking of these lives, called legal abortion, is advertised at "usually under $250." Abortions are cheap. Tragically, so is life. For a week's wages you can get rid of it.

For some lust takes precedence over the value of persons. A girl comes home late to her unlighted apartment. A young intruder forces her at gunpoint to yield to his selfish demands. Rape is followed by murder. Personhood is of less value than lust.

Life has been drastically devalued when the average fourteen-year-old American has watched eighteen thousand murders acted out on TV (as was reported through research done by Dr. Gerald Looney at the University of Arizona). Personhood has been cheapened by reading sex into everything we want to sell. Sex itself is cheapened and deadened by attaching it as a symbol to everyone. If female persons don't have a certain weight and dimension they are no-bodies. Such a philosophy has reduced God-created persons to the animal level, robbing them of personhood.

Devaluation of persons shows up, too, in the way older folks are treated. When they are no longer able to care for themselves they are carted out of comfortable houses into nursing homes to await the undertaker. Jobs, boats, color TVs, college, and a dozen other things have become more important than the lives of the elderly.

The loss of respect for human life and personhood is a tragic devaluation.

Why has human life been devalued? It has been devalued because we have lost love and respect for the creator of life — God himself. And because the giver of life has been devalued, His created people have also been devalued. How do we expect people to have respect for one another if, as some claim, man evolved from a crash in space fifty million years ago?

To give people the proper value and respect we must first give respect and dedication to the creator. Too often people put material things and their own selfish desires ahead of God. And when man fails to give God the proper place in his life, he is likely to fail in his attitude toward his fellow men as well.

What can we do as individuals to help re-establish within our society the value of human life and personhood? We can start by turning to God and really loving Him with all our heart and soul and strength, then go on loving our fellow man as ourselves and valuing persons over things.

We can choose dignity over selfishness. Women are demanding a right to choose to end life through abortion. Dignity is choosing to accept responsibility rather than demanding the end of life for another.

We can speak up publicly when we see and hear persons being devalued. If an advertiser uses sex and female persons to sell cars and other material things, you can personally call the advertiser or the dealer and express your negative response. Explain that sex and females are created by God and are too sacred and too high in value to be used to sell things. You can point out that since sex and people are sacred to you, you will not purchase a product that cheapens them. If the media and the advertiser can be convinced to give more respect to persons, it will also rub off on the public.

Another way is to use the "Readers Say" column of your newspaper to promote respect and love toward God and man. The outward acts of devaluing human life and personhood are the symptoms of the inner problem. When we see people being misused, or human life devalued, we can mention the symptom — the event — and then speak to the real inner problem through the reader's response section of the newspaper.

You can also promote the value of personhood across the line fence or on your job. Encourage your neighbor to respect his elderly mother and make her comfortable in his own home rather than giving her over to institutional care. If he is already providing for her in his home, tell him you respect him for it. Offer a helping hand, such as sitting for them, so they can go out occasionally, knowing that Mother is in good hands.

The practice of the Amish regarding old folks may offer some insights on this problem. They consider the care of their elders a priority. Grandmas and grandpas are a loved and respected part of the family. Children often have their elders live in with them, or have a "grandpa house" beside their own house.

Persons are of value because they are created by God in His image and likeness (Gen. 1:26). And God reaffirmed our worth when He gave His only Son, Jesus Christ, to die in our place in order that we might be reconciled with Him and receive the gift of eternal life.

Speak up for personal dignity and worth

at the line fence, lunch counter, and work-bench. Respect for persons must start with individuals where they live and work.

Matthew 22:37 and 39 says, "Thou shalt love the Lord thy God with all thy heart, and will all thy soul, and with all thy mind . . . . And . . . thy neighbour as thyself." Let's each do our part to help stop the tragic devaluation of human life and personhood.

15

Establishing Friendships at the Line Fence

You raise your eyes from your work. Here comes Mr. A. You drop your tools for the pleasure of meeting him. His kind, friendly voice lifts your spirits. He becomes interested in you and what you are doing. You are pleasured, honored, and at ease to have him around. His presence revives your courage and lifts your burdens.

Now meet Mr. B. At the sight of him you wonder what he wants from you now. You feel suspicious. Sometimes he is friendly — sometimes not. He greets you, yet you feel he is keeping you at arm's length. If he is friendly you question his sincerity, for you have found that his friendship is measured by what he might gain from you. He isn't interested in you or your work but sees you as an object for his benefit. He is always looking out for his own interests, such as making sure your corn doesn't sip his fertilizer underneath the line fence. So when he leaves you breathe a sigh of relief.

What makes the difference in these people? It's where their values are. What they treasure is what makes them. Whom they love molds their lives.

Mr. A is interested in others and is always ready to help those in need, though he isn't wealthy himself. Mr. B's main concern is himself and what is of benefit to him. As Jesus said, "Where your treasure is, there will your heart be also" (Matt 6:21).

Mr. A is poor according to worldly standards, but he is rich in the real things of life. He isn't dedicated to becoming wealthy, but he is interested in creating friendships, good relationships, and establishing peace with God and his fellow man. He accepts God's forgiveness for himself and returns forgiveness to his neighbor. He has many friends who love and appreciate him. When life is over he will enjoy friendship with Jesus for eternity. The rich values of this man cannot be conquered by death.

Mr. B is different. He is busy achieving. He is sharp as a hawk spotting the property line when the fence is too far on his side. He is suspicious of others; they are a threat to him. He fears they will try to cheat him out of what he feels is rightfully his own. He is uneasy in the presence of his neighbors. He gossips to one neighbor about another. He makes issues out of nothing and avoids the real issues with fabricated excuses. He has lost out on the real and meaningful things in life. His poor values will be conquered by death.

A person's love for God is expressed in line-fence behavior. How he treats his neighbor reflects his life values and his relationship with God. What is of highest importance — an extra dollar or friendship? Money and possessions are transient, but friendships may reap eternal results. Good relationships may lead your neighbor to confess Jesus as Lord.

Line-fence decision number one: Your neighbor borrowed from you and can't pay back on time. What do you do? Agonize over the interest you are losing? Take some of his prize property and say he owes it to you?

Confiscating some of his possessions may satisfy your money ego, but what will it do for your friendship? It will make things more difficult for him, as well as undermine his faith in you.

Friendship cannot be bought or sold. Going a second mile may establish an eternal relationship that an earthly price could never touch.

Decision number two: Ninety-year-old Grandpa is buried. After the funeral the relatives gather for the division of his personal effects. There is an item you desire. You feel you deserve it because you stayed overnight many times caring for Grandpa during his illness. However, your sister-in-law speaks first. What do you do?

You can insist on having the item yourself and perhaps cause alienation between your sister-in-law and yourself in the process. By taking possession of the item you might leave it for your children to fight over after you are gone. Or you can consider her feelings and be happy for her, as you see she obviously treasures the item, too. That way you'll keep a friend. And after all, aren't persons of more value than things?

Decision number three: Your neighbor is about to buy a choice piece of land from an adjoining farm. You'd like to buy it too, as you know of somewhere you can sell it at an immense profit. You know that your neighbor really needs the extra land, but you have the option of outbidding him. As he is about to close the deal, what do you do?

You can rejoice that he is able to obtain the land he needs. Or you can offer a better deal and grab it away from him. In so doing you trade friendship for monetary gain — a priceless relationship for perishable wealth. "For all the law is fulfilled in one word, even in this; Thou shalt love thy neighbour as thyself. But if ye bite and devour one another, take heed that ye be not consumed one of another" (Gal. 5:14-15).

Godly love rejoices to see his fellow man succeed. Jealousy wants the success for himself. Love helps his neighbor. Greed uses his neighbor. Love makes peace at the line fence. Greed starts a fight. Love gives himself. Selfishness takes, keeps, and hoards.

Decision number four: You are on your way to make a business deal. Sure enough, here comes that familiar car driven by the guy you've been avoiding. You pass and watch him through the rearview mirror as he drives out of sight. Later you attend a wedding and he shows up there. You call at the funeral home to offer sympathy to your neighbor who lost his father . . . and there he is.

Ever since he misused you, you have refused to speak or deal with him. You avoid him, yet it seems as though he follows you. It is such an inconvenience to have to try to avoid him all the time. You are tired, run-down, and spiritually exhausted from the years of being on the lookout for your former friend. If only he would come crawling to you on his hands and knees to make restitution for what he did. "If he would confess to me, I could go on with living."

Why carry the grudge any longer? You are hurting inside. It has made you nasty and sour all these years. The grudge lines are embedding themselves on your face. You can choose to go free. You can drop all the charges and demands.

Author David Augsburger says, "Cancel angry demands." You can choose to bear the hurt, pay the price, and be free from the deep-rooted resentment that has kept you from joyous living all these years.

The next time you see your alienated friend at the diner, slide into the booth beside him and buy him his dessert. Then and there, confess your grudge and resentments. Pull up the weeds that have keep Spirit fruit from growing in your life. Meekly and humbly tell him you are sorry for your evil attitudes. Ask him the favor of forgiveness — with no demands attached. You can then go away free.

Now you can meet him on the street with pleasure. Together you can rejoice at weddings. You can both offer honest sympathy and be free to enjoy a meal together. You can be free to enjoy living.

At the line fence people can begin working for peace in a broken world. It's a place to express the love of God within you and realize fulfillment in living.

Friendship with God and man is the most valuable possession a person can have, yet it is often replaced with something second best. Friendship is worth sacrificing for along the line fence.

16

Have a Healing Ministry of Your Own

Listen to the pulse of our society. There is something wrong! As one checks the temperature of the world's people, one must conclude that we're sick — we are in a fever — fever that calls for healing. We are constantly reminded of our sickness by the behavior of our people.

For example: In a mass slaying, seven persons were murdered in Washington. Police called it the "worst mass slaying in the city's history." When life becomes that cheap, the thermometer says we are sick.

Again I felt the heat of our fever when a friend told of her plans to leave her husband and family after many years together as a "nice" family in the neighborhood. The pain of sickness hit when I realized the unwillingness to live for others and the lack of being ashamed of such a tragic act.

While riding on a bus through Minnesota I noticed a gray-haired man reading a paperback, occasionally smiling at its content. Since I am involved with the distribution of paperbacks I wondered what he was reading and filling his mind with. He gave me one glance at the book, then quickly slid it out of sight. The pulse of society showed up again. The book wasn't fit to be seen, let alone read. With an apology he explained, "That was the best thing that was there to buy." Maybe he could have bought a dictionary, but who likes to read that to pass the time? The truth is — he was painfully near correct!

My little daughter reminded me of our sickness when she went with me to a nearby airport to restock our Christian paperback display there. She suddenly exclaimed, "Oh, Daddy, look here." Her innocent eyes had spotted the cover of one of their books showing people in the nude.

Some time later, while waiting, I leafed through some of the new stock of books. I felt sick to my stomach as I drove from the airport that day. The "stuff" people are reading is sick. We — a nation, a people — are sick!

Mother used to check us children for fever by placing her loving hand on our foreheads. If we were hot with fever she responded with healing by personally ministering to us. At our house, if one of the children has a fever the response is to become healers.

Our world has a fever. That means healers are needed!

Disciples of Jesus should see the sickness of our world as opportunities. They should grab hold of the fevers and pulses and turn them into steppingstones of healing ministries.

The people who know the Christ who saves and satisfies need to respond through a personal healing ministry. I believe every Christian should be involved in bringing hope to a sin-sick world.

Jesus said, "Ye are the salt of the earth . . . . Ye are the light of the world" (Matt. 5:13,14). Being salt and light is a personal, individual matter. I believe Jesus calls each of His followers into a personal ministry that makes life meaningful.

Take my friend who worked at the Pentagon, for example. I thanked him for the work he is doing in our book program. In return he said, "Listen, I thank you." Why did he thank me for the work he is doing? He is more than a lawyer holding a job five days a week. Now he counts. He's become a vital part of making Christian literature available to the thousands of people who work at the Pentagon. He is a part of a healing ministry.

A salesman friend pointed out to me that he sells only the "best sellers" in paperbacks. His sales figures were staggering. Then I asked, "What is your message?"

He hesitated a bit, then said, "We have no message." He was right. Our sick world has no message.

But the Christians, the Church, have a message — the message of hope and love. They should give it because it is a message of healing for the soul of man. Every Christian is called to this task.

There is a meaningful ministry for everyone.

God has a job for you to do!

There are some requirements for having a meaningful ministry. First: You cannot be ashamed of Jesus Christ. Christians repeat Paul's words in Sunday school: "I am not ashamed of the gospel of Christ" (Rom. 1:16). These words must be realized in the places where we live and work. Our lives must be profoundly clear for Jesus Christ.

While sitting at a meeting a friend leaned over and asked me, "Is that a boy or a girl in front of us?"

I said, "I don't know" — because I really didn't know. A lot of church people are like that. It's hard to tell — are they for Jesus, or aren't they? To live a life that counts, the relationship with Jesus must be personal, not a carbon copy or an echo of another Christian. You must be clearly on the side of Jesus.

A second point to a meaningful ministry: Accept yourself. If you see yourself as "Poor me, what can I do? I grew up in the sticks [or the city slum] — I'll never amount to anything," then you probably won't.

That is not you!

You are a specially designed, specially created person to do a special work at a special time — like *now*.

Many Christians would like to be a Paul or a Peter or another great person. I'm not interested. I want to be the person God meant for me to be now. I don't want to be another person at some other time. Neither do you. There is a ministry for you to accept.

Third: Be a disciple. Jesus is not just a ticket to heaven, He is a way of life. Many people would like a religion that will get them to heaven without interfering with their business or everyday life. The Jesus I know cannot be used as a first class ticket. He must be accepted as Lord and manager of life, as well as the way to life. This means our decisions will be made in relation to Jesus. Businessmen make their decisions on the basis of the dollar they gain, not on morals. The Christian makes his decisions because of Jesus. A disciple of Jesus gives up his own will and follows the will of Christ — obeying Him and His Word.

How does one begin a healing ministry? By a commitment to Christ. Tell God, "I'm Yours. I'll follow You. I'll serve You by serving others." To those who make such a commitment God gives a work to do in His kingdom. He gives them the gift and talent to do it.

Christ calls you to minister to others. The Church calls. The community calls. Lonely individuals call. Those calls are opportunities. Get started — out of a love for Jesus — and pick up on the opportunities of service around you. You'll be started in a personal healing ministry.

You can begin a teaching ministry by accepting teaching opportunities when the church calls on you. If you are not a teacher where you are, you would not make a teacher in a needy foreign field. If you are not sharing the good news of Jesus where you live,

God will hardly call you to a ministry to proclaim it worldwide. If you have no message of spiritual healing for your neighbor, you have no message for the world. If you are not faithful in little, you cannot be faithful in much. If you don't respond to God's call to serve across the street, don't expect His call to cross the ocean to take spiritual healing to a heathen nation.

Starting and developing a healing ministry begins from where you are now. If the church or community calls for your service, consider it. If lonely individuals call, listen. It may be the beginning of a dynamic ministry for your life.

One of my brothers is a hunter. During game season he brings in deer, bear, turkey, and other wild game. He even brings in moose from the Canadian northland. However, he didn't start hunting there. He started on a farm in western Maryland. When he was a boy he shaped himself a gun out of a piece of wood, fastened strips of inner tube on the front, stretched the marble-loaded strips over a trigger apparatus, and went "hunting." Did he do any good? Sure did! His homemade, inner tube-powered rifle brought in birds. He didn't decide one day that he was going to town to buy a gun and hunting suit and become a hunter. He used what he had, where he was. Today he is a hunter.

So it is in a ministry. You use what you have, when you have it, and where you have it. Then move forward as God leads you.

Our world is in need of people who will give their lives to bring healing for our ills.

17

Take Courage from John

"I feel my sins are so big God can't forgive me." These words came from a man of whom I least expected them. In fact, his words and emotions almost shook me.

He is an elder Christian brother to whom I look up, one who has walked with God for many years and is active in the church. I hadn't expected him to have such doubts as these.

But now that he has expressed his feelings in words, and I've thought it over, my appreciation for him as a brother has increased. He shared a problem common to many of us. His words reflected the doubts and questions of many Christians, though often they are not ready to admit to them.

Doesn't it seem strange that these feelings can happen to older, mature Christians? Isn't it just the young and immature ones who feel this way?

Not necessarily. Satan isn't going to miss a chance to discourage one of God's children. If a person has taken Jesus as Saviour and Lord, then the enemy will use doubt and discouragement whenever possible.

God knew we would have these problems. Forgetting God and doubting our commitments are as old as man. Adam and Eve departed from their original purpose when they yielded to Satan's invitation to doubt God's promises. Only a small number of people accepted Jesus as Messiah when He came. They lost hold of the promise. The enemy of God wants us to lose faith and feel we have no assurance. It's easy to lose hold of a promise and commitment if we don't keep it up-to-date.

God knew we needed assurance. He used the apostle John to give us a direct assurance of forgiveness of sin: "If we confess our sins, he is faithful and just to forgive us our sins, and to cleanse us from all unrighteousness" (1 John 1:9). With this assurance we can trust and need not worry.

So what happened to the elder friend who thought he was so sinful God couldn't forgive him? I don't know exactly what happened in the next twenty-four hours, but the next day he assured me everything was all right. I suspect he took some time to be alone and reclaim 1 John 1:9. If we confess, He forgives. He took care of it with God, then everything was all right.

Yes, God forgives. He promised it. When He forgives it is not held against our account any longer. God promised it. Believe it. Let that settle it.

Why bring up the problem of our elderly Christian friend? One reason is that it's a problem common to me. I have to go back to the Book of John and keep God's promise fresh and stick with it.

Another reason for bringing it up is that I believe it is a problem all Christians get a touch of now and then.

A third reason is that it's a problem most of us prefer to pretend never existed. We hide it behind false fronts, homemade smiles, Jesus buttons, and how-to-do-it courses. Then when a Christian faces this problem for the first time he feels as though he is the only person who has such doubts. That makes it difficult to get brotherly help.

The last reason for bringing it up is that you, too, may want to follow the example of getting it settled with God. You may want to keep in touch with John and get hold of the promise that "he is faithful and just to forgive." You may want to affirm to yourself: "God said it; I believe it; that settles it." You must settle it as often as the tempter brings it up.

By the way, when the feeling of sinfulness gets a hold on you, don't sink into depression. Turn it into an opportunity to take inventory. See where there may be sin, then confess it. Make every doubt turn out to be a deeper commitment for Christ.

Doubt is a common plague for the tempter to give; but it is also common for God to give the victory over it:

> There hath no temptation taken you but such as is common to man: but God is faithful, who will not suffer you to be tempted above that ye are able; but will with the temptation also make a way to escape, that ye may be able to bear it (1 Cor. 10:13).

When temptation comes you aren't alone in it. When it strikes, follow through to victory.

If Satan tempts you to think you can't be forgiven, maybe it will be valuable to you to remember the old man who also endured temptation but travailed with God and claimed the promise until everything was all right. It was a must in order for him to get on with living.

God knew we needed the encouragement of the promise He gave to us through the words of John: "If we confess our sins, he is faithful and just to forgive." Read and re-read these words. Live by them. Stand on their verdict and claim the promise. It's yours.

18

Get On with Living

I enjoy meeting people for the first time and discovering that they are fellow Christians. We have a common bond in Christ. We can fellowship together. We can discuss our beliefs with a mutual interchange of ideas. Such exchange is an uplift to the soul.

But there are those who, instead of rejoicing over our bond of brotherhood, immediately latch onto our points of difference. They try to convince me that their view is the right view. And if I don't immediately agree with them they keep on trying to convince me. It's not a matter of open discussion and fellowship — they're right and I'm blind. This same thing occurs again and again each time we meet until, finally, I don't care to meet them anymore.

A case in point: I accepted an invitation to attend a meeting at a hotel in the city. Upon arriving I was greeted by some men who asked if I had received the Holy Spirit. My answer didn't satisfy them. They wanted to know if I had the evidence of speaking in tongues. Since my answer was no, I was informed that I "didn't have it." I was told that if I had had the gift of the Spirit my first companion would not have had to pass on. I would have had the power to raise her up.

Ever since this experience years ago, that kind of people have been confronting me with their Charismatic views. If they get a chance to get started, I'm in for another playback of what I've heard dozens of times before. After some years of being "preached at," I've concluded that I must get on with *living* and leave the *arguing* to them.

Take another case, for example: Some of my friends hold the belief that once saved they cannot lose their salvation. No sin will keep them out of heaven. They are so insistent in this belief one could think God called them here to change my views. They introduce me to their friends as one who is saved but "doesn't trust Christ completely." This issue has come up dozens of times. Now when I see one of them I think to myself, "Oh no, not again!" Our visits are no longer fellowship in Christ, they are confrontations.

Case three: Regarding the end times, some Christians believe in amillennialism, others in premillennialism. If you don't come under their umbrella, you're a heretic.

I'm not sure which term my beliefs would fit under. I'll be glad to share my views in light of my understanding of the Bible, but I haven't put them down as my final, set views. When I do that, fellowship with others heads for a cutoff.

There are many issues and beliefs that can start dissension, and whenever we meet with other Christians there is a chance for confrontation. But why look for arguments? Why not try to draw out the best in each other? If both believe in the death and resurrection of Jesus, fellowship on that first. Develop faith and trust in each other on points of agreement. Instead of writing each other off and lining up the opponent for the next shot, let's build confidence in each other. Then as we learn to trust each other we can discuss differences and allow them to become growing experiences.

Does that mean I am against discussions of differences? Not at all! State your case clearly and proceed to delve into the differences as a growing experience. I'll listen to the views of others (at least twice). Then I'd like to be heard, too. When it goes from a learning fellowship to one or the other insisting on his views, we are wasting time. When someone starts praying for God to open my blind eyes, and acts as though they were the Holy Spirit convicting me of their beliefs, it's time to hop off and get on with living. When one or the other insists on his view neither person grows, but wilts away into tension and strife that kills brotherhood.

People are important. I have resolved to close no one out of my life. Yet at the sight of some Christians I have a feeling of discouragement. Instead of being a joy to meet them it's almost a dread — for here we go again with another battle of words on a busy day as they try to squeeze me into their mold.

Some would wrap Jesus into their kind of wrapper, and somewhere beneath the wrapper expect to find Jesus himself approving their thinking. Accordingly, when this kind of person comes along I'll discipline myself to listen (even if it is one of those trying persons I've heard for hours before). If there is a place in the runoff, I'll look to bring this thing to a Christ-like close so I can get on with living.

Why do I say I must get on with living? First: Life is too precious to spend it arguing over a point of disagreement. It is important what we believe. But doctrine is too sacred to be made into arguing material. Read Titus 3:9-11 for what to do when differences occur.

Second: God forbids arguing. "Do all things without . . . disputings" (Phil. 2:14). Those who continue to argue have a wrong sense of values and may be using their arguments to hide a moral twist or sin in their life. They are often dead set and closed to further truth and spiritual growth. After the argument they feel better and more righteous about their undercover sin.

Third: I'm not the Holy Spirit. My task is not to convict persons of sin nor to demand how they believe. Neither do I like others to play Holy Spirit to me. It is my task to allow God's Spirit to flow love through me to others so He can do His work. I must get on with living the Christ life, letting the Spirit work through me.

Perhaps you, too, may want to get on with living and leave the arguing to others. The man who lives life with a spirit of love and joy in Christ says more to his fellowmen than one with an argumentative "testimony." So perhaps you would like to join me in reaching to become a person who draws men to Christ by a radiant life rather than by arguing him into the "right" belief. Perhaps together we can become more like Jesus himself — acting with compassion, understanding, love, and care for others. We can be persons alive in Christ, doing His will, going on joyously living for Him. Let's get on with living!

19

Would You Feel at Home in Heaven?

Would you feel at home in heaven if you got there?

After hours of driving my family arrived at a friend's house. As we drove in the lane the door opened, and we were welcomed into the house. We felt right at home. Why? Because we knew the people who lived there. Their presence, love, and fellowship made us feel right at home.

Would you feel at home in heaven? It depends on how well you know the head Person. Heaven is being in the presence of the One who bears the marks of our sins on His hands and feet, the One who gave up

His own life for our sins at Calvary. He was buried and rose again. He went to heaven to prepare us a mansion. Heaven is being with Jesus!

Heaven! Streets of gold. Free lighting. No more sweat or toil. No war, hunger, pain, suffering, or death. No hospital bills. No undertakers. It's an endless list of benefits. However, heaven isn't heaven because of the benefits and beauty. Heaven is heaven because of who we will be with, rather than what we will have. Fellowship on earth is with people, not things. So it is in heaven — the Person makes it heavenly.

Would you enjoy heaven if you got there? Eternity is a continuation of fellowship with the master you chose to serve in life — Jesus or Satan. I doubt that the average church member could really enjoy heaven in the presence of Jesus. If you mention Jesus on the street, he calls you "so religious." Ask about a spiritual relationship with Christ and he'll tell you he was baptized. Talk about a commitment to Christ and he will inform you he is a church member. Ask for a testimony at the local jail? That's taken care of by the ministerial association. Visit the sick? That is the chaplain's job. Say grace in a restaurant? He turns red in the face. Call him to special prayer? What are you talking about?

Heaven is not the beginning of a relationship with Jesus, but the eternal continuation of an already established relationship. It will be continuing to love Jesus. Jesus called for a love with all the mind and strength. Those who love Him in this way will enjoy heaven.

It's difficult to believe that the majority of church people will enjoy heaven because they aren't accustomed to loving Jesus in the first place. They are more familiar with movie actors than with saints. They spend more time in front of the tube than in the prayer closet. They are more learned on the sports schedule than the Bible. They know more about pulling a smart deal than directing a person to Christ. They spend more time in leisure than in building the kingdom of God, and know more about the rules of business than the Sermon on the Mount. Farms, businesses, fine homes, boats, skis, and education take priority over the church. How could such hypocritical persons enjoy heaven?

The people who will enjoy heaven are the ones who gave their lives to Christ and the building of His Church. Jesus must be received as Lord of all. He is not to be used as an emergency crutch in case our plans fracture, or as an ambulance to rush to our scenes of human catastrophes, or as a free ticket to heaven, in case of an earthly exit. Can persons who use Jesus in such a manner really enjoy His presence?

There is a second reason I wonder how some people will enjoy heaven. That reason is based on our attitudes and our ability to get along with each other. Here on earth we tolerate each other and keep each other brothers-at-arm's-length, rather than loving and appreciating one another.

There are hundreds of church denominations. Many of these claim to be the final word of truth, the only true church, the way to heaven. To reach heaven you must do, talk, and act as they do. You must believe all the Scriptures according to their interpretation, and hold their view of eschatology. For those who believe they are "the ones," there may be some problems in enjoying heaven. They may have to spend eternity with some of the folks from the church down the road whom they have been bitter against for years. Or some of those "blind" folks they broke away from and battled the rest of their lives. Or some of "those" they had to wear a false smile for at the community funerals. If you really knew who might be in heaven, could you enjoy it?

How do we expect to enjoy heaven if we have no relationship with people on earth? We may be spending eternity with people we shunned.

This doesn't mean the Church breaks down her fences and lets in the goats. It means the people of God, the Church, need to have the right attitudes toward those who aren't like them. Somehow some Christians seem to think if they look right in the show window they can have evil attitudes in the storage room. Outwardly, Christians put on a sinless mask; inwardly they resent and judge those who don't do as they do.

This is not a suggestion to cheapen the biblical call to obedience. It is a call to deeper inner obedience and loyalty to Christ. This is the reason for the two points of examination of enjoying heaven: our love for Christ himself and our attitudes and love toward our fellow man.

Heaven — eternity with Jesus and those who love Him. Would you enjoy that kind of company? Whether or not you enjoy heaven depends upon whom you choose to love and serve here on earth. It will depend on whether or not you get on with truly living for Jesus here and now!